Land a Job as a
Video Game Tester

Jason W. Bay

ISBN: 0692536779
ISBN-13: 978-0692536773 (Game Industry Career Guide)

TABLE OF CONTENTS

Land a Job as a
Video Game Tester

IS THIS BOOK FOR YOU? WHY SHOULD YOU READ IT?

Are you passionate about video games? Have you wondered how you could turn your skill with games into a career as a game tester? If so, you're not alone. At my game career website, I get hundreds of questions from people that want to become game testers. Do these sound like you?

"I'm 18 and just need a job as a game tester, but **I have no idea** where to start."
– Alex

"I spend so much time and dedication playing games, I feel I should get paid! **Please send me some guidelines** to help me get started on this path."
– April

"How would I find a stepping stone for becoming a game play tester? Where I can give my **first professional attempt** to test a video game or project?"
– Nehamiah

"I can't find a single Game QA/Test job. **What should I do?**"
– Dylan

"I've wanted to test video games for some time now but I **don't know where to start** or what to look for to get into the career."
— Anthony

"I truly do have a passion for games, just **have no idea** where to truly start at. Any advice will do me some good."
— Randy

"If you could help me out, it could **change my life**."
— Colten

For people like Dylan, April and Colten starting out with no experience, it's hard to get a job for one major reason: They don't know the basics. So when they interview for a job, the company knows right away that they don't know what they're talking about — because they don't.

To make things worse, a lot of people want to become game testers, so there's major competition for each and every game-testing job in your city. When you apply to a testing job, your application will be just one in a stack of hundreds. How can you stand out?

Do you think you could get a job as a Video Game Tester if only you had the right job knowledge, knew how to build your skills, had help finding and applying for jobs, knew how to ace your interviews, and knew exactly how to succeed once you were hired?

Then you're in luck: I wrote this book for you!

This book will teach you the essentials of game testing, and help you stand out from the crowd so you can get the best job possible. I'll get you up to speed on the tools and techniques of professional game testing, so you'll be able to "talk the talk" in the job interview. I'll teach you how to write a great resume, where to find the best jobs, and how to apply. And when you land your first testing job, you'll hit the ground running because you're armed with the information in this book.

I've spent more than 15 years in the video game industry. I started as a tester and eventually became the head of a large game studio, so I know exactly what hiring managers are looking for in a job applicant.

And right now, my one and only goal is to help you land your first job as a Video Game Tester.

Your time is now. You can do this. Let's get started!

WHAT IS GAME TESTING?

Sometimes, people have the wrong idea about game testing. They think it's the same as "getting paid to play games." Hopefully you already know that's a bunch of crap – something like 60% of people play games every day, so if you could actually get paid to do that, don't you think just about everybody would be doing it?

The fires of this myth are fanned by the Internet, which we all know can be crawling with scammers. (Except for that foreign prince, who should be depositing $10 million into my bank account any day now. He seems totally legit.)

There are dozens of websites claiming they can get you a job making money "doing what you already do all day - playing video games!" That is, if you'll just pay them $49.95 to reveal the "secret." Some of them have testimonial videos that sound very convincing, while others have discussion forums full of people enthusiastically claiming that they "were skeptical at first, but they took a chance and, OMG, it really works!"

Do those websites make your spider-sense tingle? I hope so. Because those aren't game testing companies – they're scammers. So please don't give those jerks any of your hard-earned cash.

Okay then, if video game testing isn't "getting paid to play games," then what is it, exactly?

What does a game tester do?

Let's start by busting a common myth: testers do not just sit around and play games all day. Game testing is real-world work. And, like any job, sometimes it's fun but sometimes it's a stressful grind. You'll be playing games that are under construction, well before they're finished, so they'll be buggy and missing content most of the time. At the early stages, they won't even be "playable" in any real sense.

One of my tester friends describes his job like this: "I nitpick and bug the heck out of games in development with the intent to make them better." I think that's a great description, because it places all the focus on one primary goal: improving the game.

In general, testers play the latest under-construction version (called a "build") of the game, and then report anything that looks bad or doesn't work right (called a "bug" or "defect"). That's why it's called quality assurance – you're making sure that the game is high quality.

On any given day as a QA Tester, you might do things such as:

- Play the build, looking for defects

- When you find a defect, figure out how to make it happen predictably

- Type up a "bug report" (a description of the defect, along with steps to reproduce it) into special software called a "bug tracker" or "issue database"

- Submit the report to the game development team ("dev team," in testing lingo) so they can fix the problem

- The programmer that receives your report might ask for more information to help find and fix the issue

Don't worry – I'll explain every one of these steps in depth later on. For now, just keep in mind that testers try to find problems in a game, and then report the problems to the dev team to be fixed.

Why is game testing necessary?

The game tester's job is important because they're the front line of defense to make sure the game is awesome when it's released to players. If they don't do their jobs well, it can lead to millions of disappointed fans when the game ships with bugs, crashes, or (even worse) loses all of their progress. If that's ever happened to you in a game, then you know how frustrating it is.

When a game's quality assurance team does their job well, the game can turn out to be a fun *and* bug-free experience for players.

QA testing vs. playtesting

According to Wikipedia, Quality Assurance (QA) testing is "the process in which professional testers look for and report specific **software bugs** to be fixed by the development team." That's very different from playtesting, which is "the process by which a game designer tests a new game for **bugs and design flaws** before bringing it to market."

The key here is that QA testers are mostly looking for bugs, while playtesters are mostly looking for design flaws.

Playtesters are usually needed most at the end of the game development process, when the game is almost finished. But QA testers are needed by every game studio, for every game that's being made, from start to finish. And that's why it's a good job to have: As long as people are making games, there will always be demand for good game testers. (That's where you come in.)

What are some pros and cons of being a tester?

Perhaps the most enjoyable part of a job testing games, is being able to participate in the overall collaborative effort of making a game. Each day you might work with highly talented artists, programmers, designers, and leads in an effort to make the greatest game possible. It can be incredibly rewarding to watch a developing game go from a hot mess to a finished product – and to know that you played a key role in the game's success.

On the other hand, testing can sometimes be incredibly tedious work that requires a lot of commitment and attention to detail. People who land their first testing job are often surprised by how challenging the position can be. The majority of your time will be spent repeatedly testing certain features, systems, and small-to-moderate chunks of actual gameplay. Sometimes, you won't even get to play the entire game until nearly the end of the development cycle.

But I think you'll find that the pro's outweigh the con's by a landslide. Besides, even after a rough day, you'll always be able to remind yourself that you spent the day doing what you love – and the icing on the cake is that you get paid for doing it.

HOW MUCH DO GAME TESTERS GET PAID?

Whenever you're deciding on a future career, it's important to know how much the job pays when you're starting out and how much you can make later on, after you gain more experience. In this section, we look at the average salaries of testers and discuss the various factors that will affect your pay.

Tester salary data

Your salary as a video game tester will steadily increase as you get more years of experience. That's because you'll become faster at finding and reporting bugs at a higher accuracy, and that skill is valuable to employers. You'll also develop strong instincts about particular game systems, engines and platforms, so you can zero in on bugs more effectively than newbie testers that are just starting out.

One thing that's important to keep in mind: Many studios consider the game tester job to be a "non-exempt" position. At those companies, you wouldn't be on a salary like the other members of the development team. Instead, you'd be paid hourly and must be paid overtime when applicable.

Another important consideration is whether the position is full-time employment ("FTE") or full-time temporary employment ("FTT"). FTT workers generally aren't given as many benefits as FTE positions, and may not be allowed to participate in team bonus plans and other valuable perks.

Since many testing jobs are paid hourly, let's compare the wage vs. salary data.

Pay Type	Low Range	High Range
Hourly	$8.00/hour	$14.00/hour
Salary	$16,000/year	$35,000/year

Note that salaried QA positions seem to pay more per year than hourly jobs, so if you want to maximize your pay then it might be a good idea to try for jobs at companies that pay a salary rather than an hourly wage. You can find out by asking the company's Human Resources department.

Factors that affect salary

Not all testing jobs are created equal. Unfortunately, many studios treat their QA department as second-class citizens – and pay them accordingly. At others, the testing and QA groups are treated as key partners in developing video games that are stable, bug free and fun.

What I've observed is this: The studios that treat testers as an integrated part of the development teams value them more, and tend to pay them more. The studios that treat the testing group as a sectioned-off "service" group tend to pay less. They also use more contract and temporary testers and the turnover in their QA departments is higher as a result.

The numbers above are averages from many hundreds of video game tester salaries, so they're generalized. But there are other factors that can help you beat those pay averages and make more money, if you choose your employers wisely:

- **Company/studio size.** Larger companies generally have bigger project budgets, which allows them to pay their testers more. For example, GlassDoor.com shows that Big Fish Games may pay their hourly testers up to $16 per hour, which is higher than the industry average.

- **Benefits.** Some studios pay health, dental, vision and other benefits to their testers. Others don't. These perks can add up to thousands of extra dollars each year. A "total compensation statement" will itemize the dollar value of any perks above and beyond base salary. Be sure to find out about benefits before you accept any job offer.

- **Bonus structures.** For studios that choose to include their testers in the company's team or project bonus plans, a commercially-successful product could bonus as high as 40-50% extra income to a tester's base pay.

Game tester pay is certainly lower than most other jobs in the game industry, partially because testers don't need to have a professional degree like many artists, designers and programmers. But don't let that put you off, because testing is a fun and rewarding job and it's full of awesome people.

Besides, how many jobs will pay you to spend all day working with unreleased games while you get industry experience, learn all about game development, or even finish a professional degree? If you want to turn your love of games into a job, then being a QA tester is a worthwhile place to pull in a nice paycheck and start advancing your career.

CAREER ADVANCEMENT OPPORTUNITIES

If you've researched game testing on websites and discussion boards, you've probably read mixed reviews – some people say it's a good way to get your foot in the door at a game studio, and some people say it's a low-pay, "dead-end" job. Who should you believe?

I think the people that say it's a dead-end job are a bit short sighted and aren't thinking much about the future. Most any job will pay lower than other jobs in the same industry when you're first starting out, but what they're forgetting is that your pay will grow as your experience and knowledge grows. And there are other good reasons for starting your game career as a tester.

Why is QA testing a good way to start a career in games?

It teaches you about game development. Game development can be a complicated, messy, obscure process. Starting your career in QA is a great way to start learning about how game studios work and how games are made, because you see the game evolve from start to finish. You also get to meet people in every department, and that gives you a unique insight into how all the different jobs work together to make a game.

It starts building your resume. Getting experience as a game tester lets you start adding game experience on your resume, which not only helps you when you apply to future game jobs – it also builds your confidence when you network with people and employers in the game industry. Instead of being an outsider, you'll start becoming an industry insider.

It helps you build industry connections. By working at a game studio, you'll start building personal connections inside the industry. Why is that important? Because the people who are most connected get the most job opportunities. You'll start to hear about jobs before they're even posted to the public, which can really give you a leg up.

It gets your foot in the door. If you're like a lot of people starting out in games, testing might not be your dream job – maybe you hope to eventually become a game designer, programmer, or artist. It's common for people to work as game testers while they work on those other skills, and then move into a different job when a new entry-level position opens up on a game team. It's a proven strategy that works.

Can you move from testing into other game jobs?

I know many people who started as testers and then went on to become producers, artists, designers, or programmers. In fact, I started my own career as a tester and later went on to run several departments at a large game studio. But how realistic is that for you?

To give you some insight into the many career opportunities that can open up when you become a game tester, here are some examples of actual career paths taken by people I've personally worked with. Notice how they started out as testers, and then their careers progressed – sometimes into other jobs in the industry:

Kyle L. Started as a Tester > became a Lead Tester > is now a Senior Tester

Daniel S. Tester > Junior Programmer > Gameplay Programmer > Senior Engineer

Merric S. Tester > Associate Producer > Producer > Senior Producer

Jim V. Tester > Software Engineer Technician > Lead Programmer > Development Manager

Elizabeth C. Tester > Lead Tester > Associate Producer

Matt T. Tester > Associate Producer > Producer > Senior Producer > Program Manager

Brian K. Tester > Lead Tester > Associate Producer > Producer

Marc H. Tester > Programmer > Lead Programmer > Senior Software Engineer

Brian L. Tester > Associate Producer > Producer > Executive Producer

Brian G. Tester > Producer > Level Designer > Content Designer > Game Designer

Branden B. Tester > Environment Artist > 3D Artist

Allison B. Tester > Art Intern > Character Lead > 3D Designer

Jason B. (that's me!) Tester > Designer > Programmer > Lead Programmer > Technical Director > Director of Studio Operations

That's a lot of examples – and those are just the people I know! I hope that really inspires you. As you can see, some people, such as Kyle L., stayed within the testing department and built their careers by advancing into senior tester or management positions. As they advanced, their responsibilities inside the studio increased – and so did their pay rate.

Other people, including me, chose to move into a different department like art, design, or programming. We were able to do that because we got our foot in the door as a game tester, learned about the game development process, and made personal connections with people in other departments – people who were willing to give us a chance at other jobs inside the studio once we started developing skills in those areas. As you learn more skills, more job opportunities will open up for you and help secure your ongoing career in games.

JOB SECURITY

Like it or not, the video game industry is a cyclical business. Just take a look at the historical stock prices of top game companies like Zynga or Electronic Arts, and you'll see a heart-stopping roller coaster of boom and bust. Even an industry giant like Nintendo has a stock price that's swung from a low of $13 in 2005, to as much as $65 in 2007, and then back down to around $15 in 2014. If Nintendo can't maintain a steady stock price, then maybe we shouldn't expect stability from any game company at all.

Even during an industry boom, QA testing can be an unstable job. Console release cycles, big industry events like GDC, and holiday release schedules can all cause teams to load up with testers – only to lay them off or end their contracts after the big project has shipped. Unfortunately, the testing departments of game studios are often hit the hardest by layoffs during downward trends.

Luckily, there's always another game being developed just around the corner. Many QA testers regularly move between studios, and there always seems to be enough work at any time of year. Even when there aren't many testing jobs in the game industry, most QA skills transfer well to other software companies – so there's a good chance an experienced tester can get a job at non-game software companies if necessary.

It gets even easier to survive the boom-and-bust cycles if you live in a "game town" like Seattle, Los Angeles, or Austin. Cities like these ones have a large number of game studios all in the same areas, making it easier for employees to quickly land at a different company if their old company downsizes.

As long as games are being made, chances are good that you'll always be needed – as long as you're good at finding bugs. So let's get down to the nuts and bolts.

HOW TO FIND BUGS

Since the primary goal of a tester is to find glitches and errors in the game, let's start our expedition into the true art and science of the video game tester's job: bug hunting.

First of all, what exactly is a bug? A bug is any kind of flaw or mistake in the game's art, code or game play that makes it behave in an undesirable way that's not intended by its creators.

A bug could be something small, like some letters in a game menu that run outside of their button. Or it could be something major, like your character falling through the floor and into the blackness of space outside of the game geometry – forcing you to restart the level to get back on track (or to chuck your controller and ragequit).

Big or small, it's nearly impossible for a game development team to get every last bug out of any piece of software. So if you've been playing games for most of your life, you've probably encountered plenty of bugs already in released games. Even multimillion-dollar AAA games ship with bugs.

If released games have bugs, then you can bet there's 1,000 times more bugs in games when they're still under development. As a tester, it's your job to find each bug so you can report it to the dev team to be fixed.

When you hunt for bugs, there are several different methods. But the most common ones are ad hoc testing, testing against a test script, and testing for compliance. If you know about each one, it will help your chances of getting hired as a game tester. So let's take look.

Method 1: Ad hoc testing

Ad hoc testing is an informal method of testing, where you basically just play the game and run around looking for bugs in an unstructured or unplanned way. In other words, you're trying to use your knowledge of the game to think about where bugs might be likely to happen, and then you go ahead and try to make them happen.

How you do that depends on what type of game you're testing. For example, you might go into a room in the game world, shoot at the walls, jump around on the furniture, or run around the enemies without fighting them – just to see if you can make anything go wrong.

If you're concerned that you might not be able to find the bugs, don't worry! When a game is under development, there are so many bugs that it takes an entire team of QA testers to handle them all. The more time you spend testing the game, the better you'll get at thinking up new ways to find bugs.

But it can also be helpful to take a more structured approach to finding bugs, to make sure the QA team thoroughly checks every area of the game. That's where test scripts come in.

Method 2: Test scripts

While ad hoc testing is a kind of informal "guessing" about where bugs might be, a more methodical approach is to create and follow a pre-written plan of attack, called a test script or a test case.

Each test script is written and maintained by the Lead Tester, and is part of the larger testing plan. A script is just a list of predefined steps that you can take to look for bugs in a certain area of the game, in a certain way. The steps of a simple test script for a 3D adventure game might look like this:

1. Load the game

2. Use the cheat menu to skip to Level 3 ("Wall Crusher" level)

3. Move your character to stand on top of the first pressure plate in the floor

4. Ensure that the Wall Crusher is activated, and that it kills your character

This is an overly simple example, but it shows that a test script is nothing more than a list of steps that a tester can take to find out whether a small, specific part of the game works the way it's supposed to. In this case, the wall crusher is supposed to activate when the hero steps on a pressure plate, and then it's supposed to kill the hero. If it doesn't activate, or if it doesn't damage the hero, then you've found a bug.

When you load the game and perform the steps of a test script, it's called running through the script. Most game projects have a large number of test scripts – possibly hundreds or thousands of them.

And since bugs can appear and disappear multiple times while the game is being programmed, the test team may be required to run through the same scripts dozens of times during development.

Method 3: Compliance testing

You already know that video games come on many different platforms: Xbox, Playstation, Android devices, iPhones, PCs, Macs, and more. But what you might not know is that every one of those platforms has a huge number of technical requirements that a game must meet – or "comply" with. If a game doesn't comply, then the platform owner (for example, Microsoft or Apple) will not approve the game to be released on their devices.

These special rules – also called TCR's, TRC's, Lot Check requirements, and other things depending on the console maker – can be simple issues such as making sure to always capitalize the names of controller buttons in the game menus ("B Button", never "b button"). Or they could be highly technical requirements that take special hardware to discover, such as making sure the game never renders to the screen in a way that could cause seizures in sensitive players.

Forcing every game to comply with dozens of platform-specific rules might seem harsh, and it's certainly a lot of work. But it's an important way to make sure that players have a positive, consistent experience across each platform, no matter which game company developed or published the game.

When it's time to make sure the game complies with all those special rules on all the different platforms, the development team turns to the QA department to do compliance testing.

A special team within the QA department often handles compliance testing, because there's a lot of technical information the testers must understand and possibly even memorize. Each time you find a compliance rule that isn't being correctly handled by the game, you count it as a bug.

Playtesting and beta testing

Before any game is released to the general public, the developers like to make sure it's as fun and bug-free as they hope it is. That's why it's common for game companies to allow groups of normal, everyday gamers to access an "almost finished" version of their game called a beta test.

The goal of a beta test is to get the game in front of real gamers, to make sure it's fun, balanced, and stable. In exchange for early access, the players (sometimes called beta testers) agree to provide their opinions and feedback on what could be done to make the game better or more fun. The dev team can then use their feedback to improve the game.

A beta test is usually open to just a small number of players, although the definition of "small" is relative – for a massively-multiplayer online game (MMO) that's meant to eventually be played by millions, a "small" beta test could include thousands of play testers.

However, "unofficial" play testing usually starts well before the beta test. Often times, the QA team is asked to play the game and try to experience it as if they were a normal player, to provide feedback on things like "fun factor," gameplay balance, or overall look-and-feel. That's different from the usual QA job of finding and reporting bugs.

If you've already been testing a certain game for a long time as the QA tester, it can be difficult to pretend that you're an objective player with "fresh eyes" – because you already know too much about the ins and outs of the gameplay. But since most QA testers are avid gamers themselves, they can be an excellent play-testing resource for getting early feedback on a game's design before it's released to a wider playtesting or beta testing group.

For many testers, having the chance to give higher-level design and gameplay feedback can be a particularly rewarding part of the job.

Once you've found a bug using one of the major types of testing – ad hoc testing, running through test scripts, and compliance testing – then what do you do with it?

HOW TO REPRODUCE BUGS (AND WHY)

Finding bugs is a good challenge, but it's actually only the first step in the process of testing a game. The next step is that you need to be able to reproduce (called "repro," in testing lingo) the bug. In other words, you need to figure out the exact steps you took to make the bug happen, so that you can explain those steps to people on the development team.

Why would you need to explain to others how to make the bug happen, if you've already made it happen once?

When a programmer tries to fix the bug, she'll use special software (not surprisingly, called a "debugger") that will help her fix it. But there's a catch: The debugger is only helpful if she can make the bug happen again on her own workstation, while her debugger is running. So if you can't explain to her how to repro the bug, then it could be difficult or impossible for her to find the bug and fix it.

How do you repro a bug? Sometimes it's tricky. Hopefully you can remember what you were doing in the game just before the bug happened, and then you can reload the level and try to do the same things again. If you were running through a test script rather than doing ad hoc testing when you found the bug, it could be much easier to repro – because most of the steps are already described in the script. (That's another great reason to use test scripts.)

But that doesn't always work, especially if you can't remember exactly what you did to make the bug happen. Did you jump over that pit, or did you walk around? Or maybe there was something else going on in the game world that you didn't see, but is required for the bug to occur. Had an enemy walked through a door down the hallway, but you didn't notice? It can take some time and dedication to figure out.

That's why reproducing bugs is probably what you'll spend most of your time doing as a game tester. There's usually no shortage of bugs for you to find, but once you find one, it can take a focused effort to reproduce it.

I once found a bug in a Formula 1 car racing game that I was testing, which made the game freeze. But the bug only occurred because my car happened to cross the finish line at exactly the same time as one of my competitors – down to the exact millisecond. It was nearly impossible to reproduce the bug a second time, because, what are the chances of two cars finishing again at exactly the same millisecond? (Hint: not good.)

After trying to repro the bug over several races and an hour of testing, I still couldn't get two cars to cross the finish line at exactly the same time. Fortunately, the game programmer was able to look into the source code and spot the cause of the bug, even without reproducing it. I was off the hook. But it's not always possible to fix a bug without reproducing it, so I guess I got lucky that time.

Once you've found a bug and figured out how to reproduce it, it's time to tell the development team about it. You do that by writing a bug report.

HOW TO WRITE A BUG REPORT

Once you've found a bug and figured out how to reliably reproduce it, the next step is to report it to the development team. This is done using a special kind of database software called a "bug tracker" or sometimes an "issue tracker."

If you've never used database software before, don't be intimidated. It's really just a software tool to help you write a short report about your bug, and then it stores the bug on a central computer so others on the team can read it. Most bug trackers walk you through the reporting process by telling you exactly what information to provide, so it's easy to do.

Anatomy of a bug report

Different game teams will have slightly different requirements for bug reporting, but there are a few standard pieces of information that most any game team will want to know about a bug. For each of these pieces of information, the bug reporting software will provide you with a place to type it in or select it from a pre-defined list of options.

Let's take a look at the most common parts of a bug report, and how to fill them out.

1. **Title.** Give your bug a short title that summarizes what the problem is. For example, "Pressure plate on Wall Crusher level does not activate crusher, hero is not harmed."

2. **Severity.** This is usually a measure of how "bad" the bug is, often on a scale between 1 and 5. The game team will give you pointers on how to rate the severity of bugs you find – for example, they might tell you to treat art glitches as a 1 but to treat game freezes and other "showstoppers" as a 5.

3. **Assigned to:** At all times, the bug report must be "owned" by somebody. The bug report's owner will change over time, but there must always be a clear owner to be sure nobody forgets about it. Who owns the bug report at any given time? That depends on the report's Status (see below). When the report has a status like Open or Fix Failed, somebody on the development team will own it so they can work on fixing the bug. When its status is Can't Reproduce or Fixed, a tester would own it so they can provide better repro steps or verify that the bug was actually fixed. (Whenever the owner of a bug is you, the bug is said to be "in your queue.")

4. **Status.** When you create a new bug, the Status will automatically be set to Open. As the bug gets worked on and moved around between various people on the development team, its status may change to show its new state such as:

    a. **Fixed:** Somebody on the dev team is claiming that they have successfully fixed the bug. The next step would be for somebody else (usually you, if you're the tester that wrote the report) to verify that the bug is truly fixed.

    b. **Can't Reproduce:** Somebody on the team is claiming that they've tried to reproduce the bug, but they can't make it happen on their workstation using the steps you provided in your report. Often this means that the tester who found the bug needs to write better repro steps and then re-submit the bug to the dev team.

    c. **Won't Fix:** The team has decided not to fix the bug. This sometimes happens if the bug is very minor, and the developers want to spend their time fixing more important bugs. Some issue trackers have a similar status called Deferred that means they won't fix it now, but might fix it in a future version of the game.

d. **Fix Failed:** If somebody on the dev team claimed to have fixed the bug, but after regressing the bug you discover you can still make it happen, then you might set the status to Fix Failed and send it back to the dev team for another try at fixing it.

e. **Need More Info:** If the dev team has a question about the bug or needs more information from you to help them reproduce it, they might send the report back to you with a request asking for additional information.

f. **Closed:** This means the bug has been fixed, a tester has verified that the fix was a success, and the bug report can be archived. Note that the bug report might be accessed again later, if the QA team regresses it. (We'll talk more about regression testing later on.)

5. **Description:** This is the most important part of the bug report, because it's where you provide all information that might help the development team reproduce and fix the bug. It may have an in-depth description, and several reproduction steps. When you write a quality Description, it's less likely that the dev team will send the report back to you as "Can't Reproduce" or "Needs More Info."

The process of finding, reporting, and handling bugs will be slightly different from team to team, and from company to company. But the overall process will always look similar to what's described above, so this chapter is a good section to study before your job interviews.

Any game under development will contain hundreds or maybe thousands of bugs, and the test team will be required to write a report for each and every one of them. It's a big task, but you'll be surprised how many bug reports you can generate over the course of the game's development timeline. You just have to take it one bug at a time.

Tools for bug reporting and tracking

Although there are a number of different bug-tracking software packages available, most game studios use just the most popular ones. And if you learn one package, it's not hard to learn the others because they all work very much the same.

If you'd like to get a head start by practicing with some of the more common trackers now, you're in luck: many of them have free trial versions that you can use. Here are just a few:

- JIRA (www.atlassian.com/software/jira)

- Bugzilla (landfill.bugzilla.org)

- FogBugz (www.fogcreek.com/fogbugz/)

If you want some experience with a "typical" bug tracker, I'd recommend the Bugzilla link above since they offer a test database for you to play around in without having to sign up for a free trial.

HOW TO VERIFY THE BUGS ARE FIXED

When you open a bug report, the dev team will do their very best to repro the bug using the steps you specified, and then fix the bug.

But sometimes their attempt to fix it doesn't actually work. Maybe a programmer changed some code that he thought would fix the bug, but he forgot to test it in-game to make sure it was really fixed – and it wasn't. Or maybe an artist changed a character model in a way she thought would fix an animation glitch – but it didn't.

Whatever the reasons, you'll find that some portion of bugs you report will continue to be a problem even after the team has marked them as Fixed. That's why every bug report needs you and the testing team to verify that it has truly been fixed. It's the only way to be sure.

Most of the time, you can easily verify the fix: Just follow the repro steps you originally wrote in your report, and see whether the bug still occurs. If it looks like the bug has truly been fixed – yay! – then you can set the report's status to Closed and be done with it for now.

But if you try the repro steps and discover that you can still make the bug happen, then you'll need to set the report status to Fix Failed and send it back to the development team for another try. Just be sure to update the report with any new or additional info you can think of to help them fix it this time around.

HOW TO REGRESS BUGS (AND WHY)

Once a bug has been found, reported, fixed, and verified, you'd probably assume that's the last you'd ever see of that bug report. Right?

Well, not quite. Even if a bug was fixed long ago, you'll occasionally need to double-check (or triple-check, or quadruple-check) that it doesn't come back again later on. This process of checking old bugs to see if they've come back is called regression testing.

But why would a bug come back again after it's already been verified as fixed?

Because when a game is being developed, there's a lot of art, code, sound, and other components being added, tweaked, changed, reconfigured, and otherwise messed around with, by a lot of different people. As the game project grows more complicated, it becomes hard to change just one part without accidentally affecting other parts. Any change could potentially cause an old bug to reappear, or even cause what's called a "knock-on bug" – a bug that's created when a different bug is fixed.

When so many things change in the game from one day to the next, it's common for old bugs to pop up again. That's why the test team needs to do regression testing. It's the best way to test the latest build of the game to make sure the old bugs haven't crept back in to bite you.

SOFT SKILLS EVERY TESTER NEEDS

Besides being able to perform the fundamental "hard skills" parts of the job – finding, reporting, and regressing bugs – a tester must also have certain "soft skills" that help them work efficiently and effectively with their team.

There are many soft skills that can make you more successful at your job, and they may take a lifetime to truly master. But a few in particular are mentioned frequently on the game tester job boards, so let's take a look at the most in-demand soft skills so you can start working to improve them now – and mention them on your resume if applicable.

Be a gamer and love gaming

That's right: To be a good game *tester*, you need to be a good game *player*.

If you're thinking about becoming a game tester, chances are you already love video games. That's great – because if you're not passionate about playing games, and if you haven't played dozens of games across many different consoles and platforms, then you probably won't get hired as a game tester.

Why? Because video games are big, rich, complex pieces of software. They have their own technical terminology, user interface paradigms, and expected cause-and-effect behavior. You might take it for granted now, but you've probably spent thousands of hours learning how to navigate a 3D game world and become good at playing games.

Game studios don't want to spend years teaching you how to play games – they want to you hit the (virtual) ground running. So if you haven't already developed those gaming skills before you apply for a testing job, they probably won't hire you. Since you're reading this book, I'm guessing this one won't be a problem.

Team communication

Unless you're making games all by your lonesome, you'll be working with other people on a team. As the size of a game team grows from 4 people to 400, communication between the individual developers – and the different departments – becomes more complicated. So it's critical that you develop the ability to communicate with your team on an intellectual and emotional level.

To be a great team communicator, you should do your best to:

- **Listen carefully** to others on your team.

- **Ask questions** to clarify your teammates' thoughts and ideas.

- **Figure out** how others are feeling, based on their body language and facial expressions.

- **Explain your ideas** to others in a clear, concise way.

- **Express your feelings** openly, without sounding defensive or attacking others.

- **Reflect on the behavior** and activity of your team to find ways to work better together – and encourage others to do the same.

Nobody communicates efficiently all the time. And if your career is just taking off, you may have to work extra hard to be a proactive, diplomatic and effective communicator.

But your skills will improve. It just takes practice. The good news is, if you're already working to improve your communication skills all the time, then you're probably ahead of the other people applying for the same jobs.

Ownership and self-motivation

QA teams have a manager or a lead tester that assigns tasks, monitors progress, and helps train the team. But the manager can't watch over you at all times to make sure you're on task. That's why it's important for you to learn to manage your own work, and work smartly and effectively – even when nobody is looking.

There are many traits that help people take ownership of their work and become more self-motivated, but here are a few to really focus on:

- **Look beyond** your own work to try and understand the goals of the project as a whole.

- **Be energetic**, and always look for new and better ways to help the team succeed.

- **Be humble**, and don't be afraid to admit when you don't know something. (Besides, asking questions is the best way to learn new things.)

- **Be eager** to learn more about your job and your industry, and always strive to grow as a person and as a member of the company.

- **Keep a positive attitude**, and always keep an outlook of success.

- **Be persistent** and never give up – but if something doesn't work, then be creative and find another way to accomplish your goals.

- **Be focused** and stay on task, even when doing work that's repetitive or monotonous. Rise above the small stuff to always work toward the success of the project as a whole.

- **Be flexible.** You should be willing to work long hours or odd hours at times. Things change fast in the game industry, and you need to be able to adapt.

Becoming more self-motivated will definitely help you succeed in your career as a game tester, but I think you'll also find that it makes a positive difference in all aspects of your life. So start practicing to be self-motivated now, for the best chance of success later on.

Detail oriented

If you're detail oriented, it means that you pay attention to the small stuff when it matters, and you're thorough and complete in your work.

- **Be observant.** Pay close attention to everything about the game while you're testing it. Notice even the smallest of glitches.

- **Be thorough.** When writing your bug reports, be sure to give the dev team all the info they need to reproduce the bug. Use good spelling and grammar.

- **Be aware** of what's going on around you, so you can respond to the needs of teammates and the development team.

- **Stay organized.** Keep your work area clean and tidy, and figure out a good system for managing your emails and other work if necessary. Always hit your deadlines.

- **Be patient.** Take the time to do things right. Take the time to listen carefully to your managers and teammates when discussing the work.

Some people say that detail-oriented is a personality type that you're either born with or you aren't. But that's only partially true – you can become more detail-oriented just by practicing the things listed above. In fact, being a game tester for a while might just help you become more detail-oriented than you ever were before.

Technically minded

Video game testing is technical work. You'll be dealing with various kinds of hardware and software, and you'll need to figure it out quickly and become skilled in using it.

You'll also be communicating with technical people every day, such as computer programmers. In the game industry, even workers that are usually considered more "artsy" than technical – like artists and designers – can be very technically minded people.

What does it mean to be a technically minded tester?

- **Be curious.** Wonder how things work, and ask questions until you understand it. Before long, hearing the answers to all those questions will turn you into an expert.

- **Be systematic.** Approach your bug hunting in a methodical way, to make sure you test every part of the game you're working on.

- **Be scientific.** Develop theories about how the game works "under the hood," and then test your theories to see if you can find new bugs based on your hunches.

- **Be analytical.** Look for patterns to help you figure out which bugs might be related to one another, and be sure to mention them in your reports.

- **Learn technical things.** Teach yourself a few technical aspects of game development, such as programming or level design in a 3D game editor. You'll understand your job and your dev team better than ever – and it will be fun!

If you're still in school or you've never worked in a technical job like game development, it's common to be intimidated or even a little scared of the technical aspects. But trust me, you can learn it – it just takes a bit of time and effort.

WHERE TO SEARCH FOR JOBS

Now that you have a solid foundation in what a tester does and what skills are necessary, let's talk about how to find and apply for jobs.

Unfortunately, there isn't a centralized website where you can search through all the open game testing jobs. But there are three main places you can look:

1. **Company websites.** If you can think of some game studios you'd specifically like to work at, you can visit their websites (find studios by googling their names). Most have a "Jobs" or "Careers" link somewhere on the home page or sometimes on the "Contact us" page. Many studios even let you apply for the job right there on the Jobs page. To see which game studios are near your home, try www.GameDevMap.com.

2. **Job search engines.** There are a number of specialized search engines that you can use to look for jobs. Two of the best for finding video game jobs are www.indeed.com and www.simplyhired.com, because they aggregate jobs from many other job sites. Also try www.glassdoor.com.

3. **Temp agencies and testing companies.** There are testing companies and temporary-placement agencies that hire testers and then contract them out to game companies as needed. The largest might be Volt, at jobs.volt.com.

One of my tester friends has a secret for finding the best testing jobs: Search for job opportunities during the summer months, because that's when game studios need short-term QA help as they prepare to ship games in time for the holidays. Even though the job may be temporary for just a few weeks, you'll gain some hands-on experience that could help you land a permanent job later on. It's also a chance to see if you like being a tester and want to continue along that career path.

What if they require experience, and you don't have any?

Once you start looking for job openings, you'll quickly find that companies have a list of requirements that you must have in order to be considered for the job – and that most job postings say they require "prior testing experience." Many will even list the amount of experience, for example "Requires 6 months previous testing experience."

So now it seems like a catch-22: If you can't get hired without any experience, but you can't get experience without getting hired, then how can you start your career?

The answer is this: For most companies, their list of requirements contains a few items that are really more like "nice-to-haves." Job postings describe the kind of person the company would like to hire in a perfect world, but in reality they're often willing to hire candidates that come "close enough" to the ideal.

If you're not sure, follow the 80 Percent Rule: If your skills and experience meet about 80% of the requirements of the job listing, there's a good chance they'll consider you. So go ahead and apply for the job.

HOW TO APPLY FOR A JOB

After you've found some job openings using company websites and job search engines, the next step is to apply for those jobs online.

The method you use to apply will be different for different companies. Some may have an online form for you to fill out, whereas smaller studios may ask you to email your resume and cover letter to them directly. In either case, there are two important documents that you'll want to send with your application: The cover letter, and the resume.

Writing your cover letter

A cover letter is a short (less than one page) letter from you to the company you're applying to. It's your opportunity to show your passion and interest in the job and the company, and also explain how your skills and experience match up with their needs.

The goals of your cover letter should be:

- **To act as a sales pitch.** Explain to them why they should hire you by describing how your skills line up with the needs of the company. Describe how the company will benefit by hiring you.

- **To demonstrate your writing skills.** Testers do a lot of writing, so this is your chance to show your ability. Be sure to use perfect spelling and grammar! If you have trouble with that sort of thing, then ask a few friends or relatives to proofread your letter until it's perfect.

- **To show your passion.** Emphasize that you're not interested in working for just any old game company — you're specifically interested in work for *their game company*. Be sure to mention why you think their company is great and why you're excited about working there.

It will help to look at examples of good cover letters online. Just search for "cover letter examples" to get some ideas, and then customize what you find to match your own style and experience. You can view some sample game tester cover letters at www.GameIndustryCareerGuide.com/cover-letters.

Writing your resume

Your resume is the single most important document you'll create during your job search. Every job application will require it, and every hiring manager will scrutinize it when reviewing your application. It's worth spending the extra time to write a good one.

A winning resume is composed of several sections:

- **Heading.** The heading at the top of your resume should list your name, phone number, city/state, and email address. Optionally, you can include a link to your LinkedIn profile if you have one.

- **Objective.** This is a short statement describing your goals in applying for the job. Keep it brief – just 1 or 2 sentences. For example, "A position as a QA Tester supporting a talented development team making games players will love."

- **Career Summary.** This is a high-level overview of your background and skills that are applicable to the job. For example, "Passionate cross-platform gamer with strong skills in communication, attention to detail, teamwork and problem solving. Experience working with unreleased games and providing feedback as part of formal Beta Test programs."

- **Work History and Accomplishments.** This section will become the bulk of your resume. It should list the jobs you've had, the tasks you were assigned, and your major accomplishments. For each job, list the name of the company; the start and end dates of your employment there; and the 3 primary tasks you were responsible for at the job.

- **Computer and Game Skills.** This last section is a list of any computer/software skills that you have, and a list of game platforms you have experience with.

- **Honors and Awards (optional).** If you've received any academic or job-related awards that would be interesting for a hiring manager to know about you, then you can list them here. For example, if you've received an "Employee of the Month" from a past job, or made the Dean's List at a college or university.

- **Education Statement (optional).** List the names and dates of any college or university degrees or classes that you've completed.

Note that you may not need every one of these sections, so only include the ones that apply to you. If you don't have any awards or haven't attended college, that's okay – just leave those sections off of your resume.

How long should a resume be? The best resumes are no longer than one single page. Just one! If you find it's hard to fit everything on one page, then you might be adding too much detail - keep editing and trimming and condensing until it fits. I know people who have been working in games for over 20 years, and they still fit everything on one page. If they can do it, so can you.

When writing your resume, it really helps to look at some examples. To see what all these sections look like when put together into a finished resume, check out the sample resumes at www.GameIndustryCareerGuide.com/qa-resumes.

HOW TO INTERVIEW FOR THE JOB

Once you've applied for a job, the hiring manager will review your cover letter and resume. If they think they might want to hire you, then they'll contact you to schedule one or more job interviews.

For most people starting a new career, the thought of interviewing causes fear, uncertainty and doubt. But you can't get hired at your dream job if you don't ace your interviews. So it's critical to understand the process, and then prep yourself so you can nail it.

There are 2 major types of interviews: The phone interview, and the on-site interview.

The phone interview (pre-screen)

The purpose of the pre-screen interview is to "weed out" candidates that obviously aren't a fit for the job. It's usually short – anywhere from 5 to 30 minutes – and could be over the phone or via an Internet-based service such as Skype.

It usually begins with "administrative" questions to make sure you can legally work in the country and are available to start on the needed date, things like that. Then it transitions to shorter and simpler questions to find out more about your skills and background.

The interviewer will also be assessing your attitude and communication skills, so speak clearly and keep a positive attitude.

To nail your pre-screen interview, remember to:

- **Take the call in an ideal location.** Make sure your phone reception or Internet connection is solid, and your area is free from distractions: no ringing phones, no roommates barging in, no pets barking in the background or spilling your drink in your lap.

- **Review your resume and cover letter.** It's possible that you sent your application days or weeks before the call, so be sure to look them over to jog your memory in case you need to refer to them during the interview.

- **Know the company.** Play some of their games, check out their web site, and catch up on any recent articles in the news. Nothing looks worse to a potential employer than a candidate who doesn't seem to know anything about the company they've applied to.

- **Focus on the conversation.** Give all of your attention to the interviewer, their questions, and your answers. If you're the kind of person who can't help checking email or answering instant messages while you're on the phone, then avoid temptation by closing those apps before the interview starts.

The formal interview

The formal interview is what you normally think of when you imagine interviewing, so it's important to ace this one. They're done on-site at the game studio or testing company offices, and can last anywhere from a couple of hours to an entire day. It just depends on the company.

An on-site, formal interview typically looks something like this:

1   **Building tour.** They'll show you around the building or team areas. This is to "warm you up" to help you be more comfortable in the interview, but it's also an opportunity for them to sell *you* on their company. ("Isn't this place cool? Wouldn't you love to work here?")

2   **Interview sessions.** When the interview portion starts, you'll be in a conference room with a single person or a group of interviewers. This is when they ask you the "hard questions" that you'll need to prepare for ahead of time. If they ask you any questions that you can't answer, just do your best to talk through it and be up-front about what you know and what you don't. It's okay to get a few wrong, and some questions don't even *have* correct answers... they're just trying to understand how you think.

3   **Informal Q&A.** Toward the end, you may be asked if you have any questions for them. This is a great opportunity for you to ask about the studio culture, what it's like to work there, or why they like the studio. Be sure to think of a few questions before the interview – it shows them that you care.

It's important to remember that they're not just testing your hard skills – they're also assessing your personality, soft skills, and "team fit." So be sure to dress professionally and nail the interview questions while also showing them a positive attitude. Many of the interviewers are people that you'll be working with if you get the job, so be sure to present yourself as somebody they'd want to work with.

After the interviews

When you've finished going through the interview process, it's a good idea to send a "thank you" note. Don't wait – do it the very next day. Many candidates send it via email, but you can really get their attention by snail-mailing them an actual, physical card with a hand-written note of thanks.

It may take a week or more for the company to get back with you. It just depends on how many candidates they're interviewing, and how overworked the hiring managers are at the time. You should check in with your contact at the company once a week to ask about your status as a candidate.

And, last but not least, be proud of yourself! The interview process is a lot of work, and it can be stressful. Minimize your stress by understanding these different types of interviews, and by being prepared. For your best chance of success, be sure to study the bug hunting and the soft skills sections of this book.

ACCEPTING A JOB OFFER

After you've applied to a job and finished interviewing with the hiring team, the payoff will come when the company decides to hire you and makes you a formal job offer.

What's in a job offer?

A job offer is usually a formal letter, along with a legal contract that you will sign if you agree to take the job. Read the contract carefully, because it contains information that is very important about the job, including things such as:

- What your job title will be if you accept the job

- The wage or salary they are offering you

- The health benefits they will provide you (if any)

- The project-based or annual bonus pay they offer (if any)

- The amount of holiday and vacation time off you'll receive each year

- The date they want you to start working at the job if you accept it

Besides the items listed above, there are other considerations that you might have to ask about before making a decision. You'll especially want to find out whether the job is full-time or temporary.

Full-time vs. Temporary jobs

When you're searching for testing jobs, an important factor is whether the position is full-time employment ("FTE") or full-time temporary employment ("FTT"). FTT workers generally aren't given as many benefits as FTE positions, and may not be allowed to participate in team bonus plans and other valuable perks.

Also, many studios consider the game tester job description to be a "non-exempt" position. That means they're not on a salary like the other members of the development team. Instead, they're paid hourly and must be paid overtime when they work over 40 hours in one week.

That may sound great at first, because you could make a lot of extra overtime money during "crunch times" when the game team is working long hours to ship a build. But all overtime must be pre-approved by a manager – and since projects are often on a tight budget, overtime may be denied. So instead, you have to work more rigorously than you typically would in a normal 40-hour week. Not fun!

When you're comparing testing jobs at different companies, be sure you're comparing apples to apples by finding out whether each job is FTT or FTE, and whether they treat their permanent QA staff as exempt or non-exempt. Ask the studio's recruiter or human resources person if you're not sure.

Should you accept the offer?

Congratulations on getting a job offer! But don't jump on the very first offer you get - now it's time to decide whether you really want this job, or whether you should hold off for a better offer from another company.

Before accepting the job offer, you may want to ask yourself these questions:

- After doing the interviews, does the company still seem like a place you really want to work?

- Do the job requirements fit your lifestyle needs? For example, do the hours and the office location work for you and (if applicable) your family?

- Is the salary they're offering competitive for your area, or are they offering too little? Does it fit with your personal budget needs?

- What does their benefits package include, and when would you start receiving the benefits?

- Are you genuinely excited about the job? Will taking this job help you grow and advance your career?

If you're not sure about any of these questions, it's okay to call or email your contact at the company to ask questions or get more information. For example, you might want to ask them for a detailed job description if they didn't include one in the offer letter.

Most job offers will give you a week or two to make your decision. Before you accept any offer, don't be afraid to take some time and really contemplate whether the job is right for you.

If all of the things the company is offering you look good and you want to accept their job offer, then follow their instructions to sign the contract and return it to the company.

Remember that the job offer is a legally binding contract, so if you're unsure about anything at all then you should get help from a law advisor before signing.

CONGRATULATIONS!

If you've made it this far, then you've come a long way – and you're much, much closer to landing the job you've always wanted.

Shigeru Miyamoto, the game designer who created some of the most influential games of all time, once said:

"I think that inside every adult is the heart of a child. We just gradually convince ourselves that we have to act more like adults."

That may be what I love most about people who work in the video game industry: They've continued to nurture the imagination, sense of adventure, and childlike heart they've had since they were young. I have a feeling you might be like that, too.

Armed with the information you've just read, I hope you're more confident than ever before that you can land your dream job as a Video Game Tester. Now get to work, because the sooner you land that first job, the sooner you'll begin bringing countless hours of imagination and adventure to those childlike hearts all around the world.

Your future in games starts today!

JASON W. BAY

APPENDIX A: FREQUENTLY ASKED QUESTIONS (FAQ)

Do I have to go to college or university to become a video game tester? What kind of degree should I get?

QA testing is generally considered an entry-level position in the game industry. Most companies do not require a college degree to be hired as a game tester. But if you do get a degree, then you have a much better chance of moving into higher-paying jobs in QA, or moving into other areas of game development like art, design or programming. To be honest, those other jobs almost always pay a lot more than a job as a tester. So if you want to have a *career* in the game industry and not just a *job* then it's smart to seek out an education.

In fact, many of the testers I've known over the years were working as testers so they could pay their way through college. They would work part time while they went to school, or even full time while they took classes in the evenings. (Many colleges have "evening degree" programs for working professionals.) Then, after they got their degrees, they got a new job, sometimes at the same studio, doing what they went to school for – like art, programming or design. And you can bet they also got a healthy pay increase.

Do I need to move to a certain location to be a video game tester?

Most game testing jobs are going to be near the larger game studios, in the larger cities. If you want to break into the game industry, you'll eventually want to move to one of the major game development towns. For example Seattle, San Francisco, L.A., Austin, or New York. However...

Can I get a job testing video games from home?

I don't personally have experience with "work from home" testing companies, but they do exist. I asked one of my friends who has run several

QA groups over the years. He said he's received positive recommendations for Applause (formerly uTest). They provide a "crowd-sourced" testing service, and he thinks that many of their QA employees work from home.

There are some companies (for example, VMC) that you can sign up with to do a bit of from-home Beta those are likely not full-time "jobs" – just a couple hours a month if they even call you. Any other site that claims you can work as a full-time tester from home is likely a scam. There are some very convincing scams out there – they show up on page 1 of Google searches, they have testimonial videos that seem legit, but they're not. Never give any company money to apply or to sign up for a job.

Where would I find someone hiring for video game testers?

You could start by searching some of the major video game job boards. There's a good list at the game job resource page at www.gameindustrycareerguide.com/jobs.

What high school classes or after school activities would be great for video game testers?

Can I assume that you already love to play games? If so, start paying attention to the bugs in each game. Learn how to "break" the game by doing things inside the game world that the designers didn't expect you to do. Also, to be a good tester you need to be disciplined and focused. Pay attention in school and get good grades.

You can also learn more about game design by reading through some of the top game design books. Start by exploring the books recommended by top game designers, listed at www.gameindustrycareerguide.com/best-video-game-design-books.

Some classes that could help you get a QA job might be: technical writing, computer programming (introduction), project management, possibly Microsoft Excel.

Are game testers required to travel once in a while?

Normally, testers don't have to travel much. But it depends on what kind of company you're working for. If you end up being a tester on a project that's developed in a different town than where you're testing it – for example if you're working for a publisher in San Francisco but the developer is in Seattle – then you might need to travel occasionally. If you can't travel for some reason, it's probably not a deal-breaker for most testing companies.

What other kinds of testing jobs are out there?

There's also a job that you may not have heard of yet, called an "SDET." That stands for "software design/development engineer in test." It's a cool job that's basically a programmer that writes code – code that tests the game in an automated way. So it's like a testing job, but the salary is much higher since it requires programming skills. A programming degree or some programming classes would be really helpful for landing a job as an SDET.

What kinds of companies would be good to work for?

That's really up to you. What kinds of companies do you like? Which games and types of games are your favorites? Which companies are in cities that you think you'd like to live in?

A good set of rules to help with a decision might be:

4   Work at a company that makes games you're interested in. You'll be spending a lot of time testing their games. It will be more fun and engaging if you like what you're working on. You won't always get to work on stuff you love to play, but do it whenever you can.

5   Work at a company that's big enough to have different career options for you. You probably won't want to stay in the same job forever. Try to work at a company that has several teams and several products, so you can have a chance to move up or change jobs after a few years.

6   Work at a company that has friendly, fun, nice people working there. You may be working very long hours for days or weeks before each game release. It will be much more enjoyable if the people you're working with aren't jerks.

How old do you have to be in order to be a video game tester?

Technically, you just need to be whatever the minimum working age is in your state/province. But many game companies won't hire people as testers until they turn 18 years old.

Do testing companies provide health insurance and other benefits?

No, not all companies provide insurance to QA testers. Many companies hire QA as "temporary" workers, and are not required to pay for their health benefits. If a tester is employed through a temporary staffing agency, the agency may pay health insurance. Otherwise you should buy private insurance for yourself.

Do video game testers get bonuses like for Christmas or other holidays, and if so how much?

That depends on the studio you work for. Some studios give bonuses, and some don't. For companies that do give bonuses, it's usually based on the success of a shipped product or it could be based off of the studio's revenue for the past year. Bonuses are usually a percentage of your annual salary, anywhere from 5% on up.

Do video game testers get vacations? If so, how long, and are you paid during vacations?

If you're hired as a full-time employee, you'll normally start accruing paid vacation time right away. Temporary employees do not usually get paid vacation.

Do the companies give you the game systems that you need to work with or do you need to buy them yourself?

The game companies will provide the game systems. Often, you'll be using a "dev kit" version of the game system, which is a specially modified version that allows developers to debug their games as they create them. Only official game studios have access to dev kit hardware, so they will provide the kits to their employees.

APPENDIX B: INTERVIEW WITH PROFESSIONAL GAME TESTER BILL SCHNEIDER

Bill Schneider is a professional video game QA tester. He's been testing games for over a decade, and you can see his name in the credits of over 40 shipped titles – everything from Harry Potter to The Sims, and from Bejeweled to Assassin's creed. Let's find out how his career has taken him from a front-line game tester, to a manager and leader of entire testing teams at major game studios.

What do you do each day as a Video Game Tester?

The most generalized overview of my daily responsibilities would be "I nitpick and bug the heck out of games in development with the intent to make them better."

Actually, in my current job as a Game QA Lead, I coordinate with the production and development teams to organize, plan, and supervise testing efforts on a specific title from start to finish... and beyond. (Live Operations).

How did you start your game testing career?

It's a long, sordid tale full of high aspirations and broken dreams... but to be perfectly honest, I sort of fell into it.

I graduated college with the intent of being a Network Administrator, but the timing couldn't have been worse as the "dot-com bubble" had recently burst and tech companies were in major hiring freezes.

Unable to land a job in my chosen career, I made ends meet by doing temporary administrative work at various places when a friend contacted me about a full-time testing job at a 3rd-party game development studio where he worked. Having been a long-time gamer, I gave it a shot and, as luck would have it, was hired within an hour of the interview. Since that day, I've been in QA as a tester, lead, or manager and never looked back.

What do you like most about being a Game Tester?

I really enjoy participating in the overall collaborative effort of making games. Each day I work with groups of individual contributors, development leads, and product owners. We all share information with each other, constantly look for ways to streamline process, remove obstacles, and ultimately try to make the best game possible.

The success of a game isn't really up to us, but the idea of putting forth our best efforts to create something in a medium we all enjoy, can be incredibly fulfilling.

What's your least favorite part?

The least favorite aspect of my job is reminding people outside our discipline that testing and quality assurance is an integral part of the development process.

As QA is often not physically located with development teams, it's important to me they are viewed as part of it. Testers are thoughtful and talented sources of information and contributors of ideas and effort; their presence should be included in team or company meetings and events, but they tend to be overlooked or forgotten (whether accidentally or otherwise).

What aspects of the Game Tester job might surprise people?

Being a game tester doesn't mean we just sit around getting paid to play games all day – it's not the best (or easiest) job in the world. The reality is this: Testers play games all day that are unfinished, unbalanced, often incredibly broken. We'll play the same broken game over and over every day, sometimes overnight and on weekends for months – and possibly even years, depending on the game.

It can be incredibly tedious work that requires a lot of commitment and attention to detail. People who land their first testing job are often surprised by how challenging the position can be. The majority of our time is spent repeatedly testing certain features, systems, and small-to-moderate chunks of actual gameplay. Sometimes, we don't get to play the entire game until the nearly the end of the development cycle.

Also, while the terms are often used interchangeably, there is an actual difference between "testing" and "quality assurance:"

- **Testing** is about producing quantifiable results by running test passes on features and systems, focusing on bug counts, trends, and burndown rates (the rate at which the team fixes bugs) to make the game as "bug-free" as possible by the end of the testing cycle.

- **Quality Assurance** centers on user experience and satisfaction, usually through gameplay audits (or "playtests"), competitive analysis, balance testing, or other aspects that may affect the intended audience's overall enjoyment of a game.

What does it take to succeed as a Game Tester?

As mentioned previously, discipline and attention to detail is important. Basic knowledge of technical writing is helpful, as the bugs we write need to be easily understood, detailed, and precise, yet brief.

I would also encourage those who are creative, tinkerers, and naturally curious to try their hand at testing, as "outside the box" thinking and people who like finding out how things work and solving problems would be successful testers. I've also found that patience and a good sense of humor goes a long way in this job.

Surprisingly, you don't have to be a hardcore gamer to be a good tester – some of the best I've worked with were casual gamers.

What advice would you give to somebody thinking about a career testing games?

Look for testing job opportunities during the summer months. Game studios may need some short-term QA help during that time as they gear up for the holiday push. Not only will you gain some hands-on experience, it's a chance to see if testing is a good career path for you. There are some good online resources like forums and LinkedIn communities you can check out. Also, talk to any friends or acquaintances that have worked in the industry.

Take some professional/business writing and communication classes, which I believe to be valuable in any career, but will serve you well in QA. If you're looking to move beyond the tester role and into management or another discipline, I strongly recommend earning a Bachelor's Degree, as it has become heavily considered by recruiters and hiring managers.

You can connect with Bill via his LinkedIn profile at www.linkedin.com/in/schneiderwt.

ABOUT THE AUTHOR

Jason W. Bay is the creator of the Game Industry Career Guide website, where he publishes insider information and inspiration to help thousands of aspiring game developers start and build their careers.

Jason has spent over 15 years in the video game industry in many roles including tester, designer, writer, programmer, technical director, and director of studio operations. He's been a featured presenter at international game industry conferences, written for industry magazines, and worked with top game development schools to help students get hired.

Connect with Jason on Twitter @YourGameCareer, or swing by his career website for a ton of free info about game industry jobs at: www.GameIndustryCareerGuide.com.

23279233R00034

Printed in Great Britain
by Amazon